TODAY I ASKED GOD
TO REMIND YOU THAT
YOU

matter.

HE'S ABSOLUTELY
CRAZY ABOUT YOU.

*But to all who did receive him,
who believed in his name, he gave the right
to become children of God.*

JOHN 1:12 ESV

**Free yourself from the many titles you have
and the multitude of tasks on your plate today,
and do something that brings you joy.**

MELISSA HORVATH

For more
inspiration,
scan here:

I PRAY YOU WILL

never

FORGET THAT YOU'RE AN OVERCOMER. WITH GOD'S HELP, YOU CAN MAKE IT THROUGH.

For everyone born of God overcomes the world. This is the victory that has overcome the world, even our faith. Who is it that overcomes the world? Only the one who believes that Jesus is the Son of God.

I JOHN 5:4–5 NIV

Don't try to do it on your own—
let Him work through you
to make all things good.

MELISSA HORVATH

For more inspiration, scan here:

I ASKED GOD
TO BRING YOU
peace
TODAY,
IN PLACE OF STRESS.
(HEY, YOU'RE TOO BLESSED
TO BE STRESSED!)

Do not be anxious about anything,
but in everything by prayer and
supplication with thanksgiving
let your requests be made known to God.

PHILIPPIANS 4:6 ESV

Even in times of stress, God provides.
When negativity starts creeping in,
turn stressful thoughts
into remembering the blessings.

MELISSA HORVATH

For more inspiration, scan here:

I PRAY THAT
YOU WILL FIND WAYS
TO GO EASY ON
YOURSELF, TO GIVE
YOURSELF SOME
MUCH-NEEDED

grace.

Let us then approach God's throne of grace with confidence, so that we may receive mercy and find grace to help us in our time of need.

HEBREWS 4:16 NIV

Practice grace today—
not only with yourself but with others too.

MELISSA HORVATH

For more
inspiration,
scan here:

I PRAYED THE LORD WOULD REMIND YOU THAT YOU ARE *uniquely* MADE—FOR A REASON! DON'T TRY TO BE LIKE THE OTHERS. JUST BE THE BEAUTIFUL BEING GOD MADE YOU TO BE!

For you formed my inward parts; you knitted me together in my mother's womb. I praise you, for I am fearfully and wonderfully made. Wonderful are your works; my soul knows it very well.

PSALM 139:13–14 ESV

Instead of looking outwardly and comparing yourself to others, look inwardly and see what you need to celebrate!

MELISSA HORVATH

For more
inspiration,
scan here:

I PRAY THAT YOU COME TO REALIZE YOU ARE ALREADY A

SUCCESS

IN GOD'S EYES. HE DOESN'T COMPARE YOU TO ANYONE ELSE.

Depend on the LORD in whatever you do,
and your plans will succeed.

PROVERBS 16:3 NCV

Remember, everyone and every family
has their own struggles,
whether people know about them or not.
Rest in the peace that God brings,
knowing that He made you, you!

MELISSA HORVATH

DaySpring

For more
inspiration,
scan here:

TODAY I PRAYED THAT GOD WOULD REMOVE ANXIETY FROM YOUR HEART. TAKE A DEEP BREATH, COUNT TO TEN, AND BE FILLED WITH HIS

peace.

"I have said these things to you,
that in me you may have peace.
In the world you will have tribulation.
But take heart; I have overcome the world."

JOHN 16:33 ESV

Give your stresses to God and live His grace. You'll end up finding that you can face each day, no matter how busy, with an inner peace of thankfulness.

MELISSA HORVATH

For more
inspiration,
scan here:

I PRAYED FOR GOD TO REMIND YOU THAT GOOD THINGS COME TO THOSE WHO

For everything there is a season,
and a time for every matter under heaven.

ECCLESIASTES 3:1 ESV

We're working for God, not for us.
Waiting is not wasting
when you're waiting on the Lord.

MELISSA HORVATH

For more
inspiration,
scan here:

I PRAYED THAT GOD WOULD REMIND YOU THAT HE HAS EVEN *bigger* PLANS FOR YOU THAN YOU HAVE FOR YOURSELF. YOU CAN TRUST HIM!

For I know the plans I have for you, says the Lord.
They are plans for good and not for evil,
to give you a future and a hope.

JEREMIAH 29:11 TLB

Keep praying and seeking God's voice,
and He will unveil His plans for you.
Hang in there!

MELISSA HORVATH

DaySpring

For more
inspiration,
scan here:

I ASKED GOD
TO REMIND YOU
THAT YOU CAN

Keep going,

EVEN IF YOU
DON'T FEEL LIKE IT.
YOU'RE NOT STUCK.

*Let us not become weary in doing good,
for at the proper time we will
reap a harvest if we do not give up.*

GALATIANS 6:9 NIV

If you're feeling stuck and unsure
about changing your path, take it to the Lord.

MELISSA HORVATH

For more inspiration, scan here:

I PRAY THAT YOU ARE REMINDED OF YOUR

value

TODAY. YOU ARE MORE PRECIOUS THAN RUBIES, MORE VALUABLE THAN EVEN THE MOST EXQUISITE DIAMOND RING!

"Are not five sparrows sold for two pennies?
And not one of them is forgotten before God.
Why, even the hairs of your head are all numbered.
Fear not; you are of more value than many sparrows."

LUKE 12:6–7 ESV

You were created by the One who created the universe—how wonderful is that?

MELISSA HORVATH

For more
inspiration,
scan here:

TODAY I PRAYED FOR GOD TO REMIND YOU THAT HE HAS A PLAN AND A *purpose* FOR YOU.

*And we know that
for those who love God
all things work together for good,
for those who are called
according to his purpose.*

ROMANS 8:28 ESV

The next time a stressful thought enters your mind, recall the good the Lord has done for you—even the smallest things like the shoes on your feet or change in your pocket.

MELISSA HORVATH

I ASKED GOD TO REMIND YOU THAT HIS TIMING IS

perfect.

WHATEVER YOU'RE WAITING FOR, TRUST HIM IN THE WAITING.

Wait for the LORD*;*
be strong and take heart
and wait for the LORD*.*

PSALM 27:14 NIV

Don't always look for what's next;
it will be revealed to you in its own time,
in God's time.

MELISSA HORVATH

DaySpring

For more inspiration, scan here:

I SAID A PRAYER
FOR YOU TODAY,
THAT YOU WOULD BE
REMINDED OF GOD'S

nearness.

HE'S SO CLOSE,
YOU COULD REACH OUT
AND TOUCH HIM.

The LORD is near to the brokenhearted
and saves the crushed in spirit.

PSALM 34:18 ESV

If you wish to be able to discern
your inner voice from the Holy Spirit,
pray for God to reveal Himself to you
so that you can hear His plans for you.

MELISSA HORVATH

For more
inspiration,
scan here:

YOUR LIFE HAS A PURPOSE. I HAVE PRAYED FOR YOU, THAT YOU WOULD SEE YOUR LIFE AS A GRAND

adventure!

God has made us what we are.
In Christ Jesus, God made us to do good works,
which God planned in advance
for us to live our lives doing.

EPHESIANS 2:10 NCV

When you say yes to God's plans,
you're saying yes to a great adventure.
He won't leave you. He'll walk you through it!

MELISSA HORVATH

For more
inspiration,
scan here:

I'M PRAYING YOU WILL BE REMINDED THAT YOU CAN MAKE IT THROUGH THE STORMS YOU'RE GOING THROUGH. THE ONE WHO

calms

THE STORMS LOVES YOU.

[The LORD] will be a shelter
and shade from the heat of the day,
and a refuge and hiding place
from the storm and rain.

ISAIAH 4:6 NIV

Put your full faith and trust in God,
and He will equip you
and see you through any storm.

MELISSA HORVATH

For more
inspiration,
scan here:

TODAY
I LIFTED YOU UP
IN PRAYER
AND ASKED GOD
TO SHOW YOU HIS
special plans
FOR YOUR LIFE.

Many are the plans in the mind of a man,
but it is the purpose of the L*ORD* *that will stand.*

PROVERBS 19:21 ESV

God already wrote your story before you were born, He knows what's best for you, and His story for you is better than you could ever imagine.

MELISSA HORVATH

For more
inspiration,
scan here:

I PRAYED FOR YOU
TO EXPERIENCE

peace

TODAY,
AND THAT YOU WOULD
NOT BE OVERCOME
BY FEAR.

I sought the LORD,
and he answered me
and delivered me from all my fears.

PSALM 34:4 ESV

If you feel broken, scared,
and down a road you can't turn around in, pray.

MELISSA HORVATH

For more
inspiration,
scan here:

I PRAYED FOR YOU JUST NOW AND ASKED THE LORD TO REMIND YOU THAT YOU ARE CAPABLE OF DOING

hard things,

EVEN IF YOU DON'T FEEL LIKE IT.

You, dear children, are from God and have overcome them, because the one who is in you is greater than the one who is in the world.

I JOHN 4:4 NIV

It's hard to leave situations that are comfortable to pursue God's plans for us. But when He says to move, move.

MELISSA HORVATH

For more
inspiration,
scan here:

I PRAYED FOR YOU TODAY, THAT GOD WOULD GIVE YOU

answers

TO THE QUESTIONS YOU'RE ASKING.

"Call to me and I will answer you,
and will tell you great and hidden things
that you have not known."

JEREMIAH 33:3 ESV

God's work has just begun.

MELISSA HORVATH

DaySpring

For more inspiration, scan here:

TODAY I'M PRAYING FOR YOU, THAT YOU WILL BE

victorious

IN ALL YOU DO.

"So no weapon that is used against you will defeat you. You will show that those who speak against you are wrong. These are the good things my servants receive. Their victory comes from Me," says the LORD.

ISAIAH 54:17 NCV

God tends to send help in many different ways, so be on the lookout.

MELISSA HORVATH

For more inspiration, scan here:

TODAY I ASKED GOD TO REMIND YOU THAT HE HAS PLACED

special gifts

AND ABILITIES INSIDE OF YOU.

We all have different gifts,
each of which came because of
the grace God gave us.

ROMANS 12:6 NCV

What we may not have uncovered yet is the ability to use competition to empower one another.

MELISSA HORVATH

DaySpring

For more
inspiration,
scan here:

TODAY I PRAYED FOR YOU AND ASKED GOD TO

provide

FOR ALL OF YOUR NEEDS—PHYSICAL, MENTAL, EMOTIONAL, AND FINANCIAL.

And my God will supply every need of yours according to his riches in glory in Christ Jesus.

PHILIPPIANS 4:19 ESV

If God has given you the gifts and is moving your heart in that direction, He will provide.

MELISSA HORVATH

For more
inspiration,
scan here:

I PRAYED FOR YOU JUST NOW AND ASKED GOD TO REMIND YOU THAT YOU ARE

His child,

LOVED BY HIM WITH AN EVERLASTING LOVE THAT DEFIES COMPREHENSION!

The Father has loved us so much that we are called children of God. And we really are His children. The reason the people in the world do not know us is that they have not known Him.

I JOHN 3:1 NCV

God loves us, He treasures us, and He delights in our existence.

MELISSA HORVATH

DaySpring

For more inspiration, scan here:

I SAID A PRAYER FOR YOU TODAY, THAT YOU WOULD SEE THE CHANGES IN YOUR LIFE IN A POSITIVE LIGHT.

New beginnings

CAN BE BEAUTIFUL!

"Remember not the former things, nor consider the things of old. Behold, I am doing a new thing; now it springs forth, do you not perceive it? I will make a way in the wilderness and rivers in the desert."

ISAIAH 43:18–19 ESV

It's so hard for us planners to change course, but you know what's better than planning? The freedom of knowing that God has the sails.

MELISSA HORVATH

For more inspiration, scan here:

GOING THROUGH A DRY PATCH? TODAY I PRAYED THAT GOD WOULD POUR OUT

His love

ON YOU IN NEW AND FRESH WAYS.

But God shows his love for us
in that while we were still sinners,
Christ died for us.

ROMANS 5:8 ESV

During these times,
it's important that we remember
to turn to Jesus for the life-giving water
that only He provides.

MELISSA HORVATH

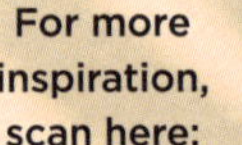
For more
inspiration,
scan here:

TODAY I PRAY
YOU'LL FIND THE TIME
TO PRESS THE

pause

BUTTON!

In peace I will
both lie down and sleep;
for you alone, O LORD,
make me dwell in safety.

PSALM 4:8 ESV

We all need to step away
from the roles we are in
and take a minute to remember
who we are and whose we are.

MELISSA HORVATH

For more
inspiration,
scan here:

I SAID A PRAYER THAT YOU WOULD

not be overwhelmed

BY THE LITTLE IRRITATIONS TRYING TO GET TO YOU TODAY.

Be patient, then, brothers and sisters,
until the Lord's coming. See how the farmer waits
for the land to yield its valuable crop,
patiently waiting for the autumn and spring rains.

JAMES 5:7 NIV

Even if you make a wrong turn,
God won't forsake you.

MELISSA HORVATH

DaySpring

For more
inspiration,
scan here:

I ASKED GOD
TO REMIND YOU THAT
IT'S OKAY TO

say no!

YOU CAN USE THAT WORD
WITH CONFIDENCE.

*But if any of you needs wisdom,
you should ask God for it.
He is generous to everyone and will give you wisdom
without criticizing you.*

JAMES 1:5 NCV

If you feel in your soul that something isn't right,
maybe God is preparing you to move on to what is next.

MELISSA HORVATH

DaySpring

For more inspiration, scan here:

I SAID A PRAYER
FOR YOU TODAY,
THAT YOU WOULD

slow down

LONG ENOUGH TO STOP
AND SMELL THE ROSES.
(THEY'RE LOVELY,
BY THE WAY!)

Then Jesus said, "Come to Me, all of you who are weary and carry heavy burdens, and I will give you rest."

MATTHEW 11:28 NLT

While you're resting, don't forget to listen. It's often in these kinds of times when God speaks to us, when His nudges come and our purpose grows.

MELISSA HORVATH

For more
inspiration,
scan here:

IS THE WORLD CRASHING DOWN ON YOU TODAY? I PRAYED THAT GOD WOULD REMIND YOU THAT HE OWNS THE WHOLE WIDE WORLD AND CAN

handle

WHATEVER YOU'RE FACING.

"Fear not, for I am with you; be not dismayed, for I am your God; I will strengthen you, I will help you, I will uphold you with my righteous right hand."

ISAIAH 41:10 ESV

Have faith that God is already taking care of you and knows your next steps.

MELISSA HORVATH

DaySpring

For more
inspiration,
scan here:

TODAY I ASKED GOD TO REMIND YOU THAT HE'S

still speaking

TO YOUR HEART, EVEN WHEN YOU THINK YOU CAN'T HEAR HIM.

"My sheep listen to My voice; I know them, and they follow Me. I give them eternal life, and they will never die, and no one can steal them out of My hand."

JOHN 10:27–28 NCV

If you feel as if you haven't heard from God, pray that He will reveal Himself to you.

MELISSA HORVATH

For more
inspiration,
scan here:

TODAY I PRAYED THAT YOU WOULD REMEMBER THAT GOD IS *fighting* YOUR BATTLES FOR YOU. REST EASY, WARRIOR.

All those gathered here will know that
it is not by sword or spear that the LORD *saves;*
for the battle is the LORD*'s,*
and He will give all of you into our hands.

I SAMUEL 17:47 NIV

Release everything you have hanging over your head and take delight in being a child of God.

MELISSA HORVATH

For more
inspiration,
scan here:

I ASKED GOD TO REMIND YOU TODAY THAT HIS IS THE

only

OPINION THAT MATTERS.

The LORD is my strength and my shield;
in him my heart trusts, and I am helped;
my heart exults, and with my song
I give thanks to him.

PSALM 28:7 ESV

You can always come and talk to God—anytime, anywhere, and about anything. He is always listening.

MELISSA HORVATH

For more
inspiration,
scan here:

I PRAYED FOR YOU TODAY, THAT YOU WOULD SEE LIFE AS A

celebration!

This is the day that the LORD has made;
let us rejoice and be glad in it.

PSALM 118:24 ESV

God longs to celebrate your victories with you, so remember to thank Him and give Him the credit He is due.

MELISSA HORVATH

For more inspiration, scan here:

TODAY I ASKED GOD
TO REMIND YOU
THAT HE IS
big enough
TO HANDLE ALL
THAT YOU'RE GOING
THROUGH.

Great is our Lord, and abundant in power;
his understanding is beyond measure.

PSALM 147:5 ESV

If we take the first step to love one another, messes and all, realizing that everyone is different, we can start living like Christ.

MELISSA HORVATH

For more
inspiration,
scan here:

I PRAYED FOR YOU
TO BE REMINDED THAT
GOD IS IN THE
DIY BUSINESS, MAKING
OLD THINGS INTO

new.

If anyone belongs to Christ,
there is a new creation.
The old things have gone;
everything is made new!

II CORINTHIANS 5:17 NCV

A table is being prepared for you,
and even though it's hard to wait, it's so worth it.
God's work has just begun.

MELISSA HORVATH

For more
inspiration,
scan here:

TODAY I PRAYED
THAT GOD WOULD
REMIND YOU THAT HE
loved
YOU ENOUGH
TO GIVE HIS VERY LIFE
FOR YOU.

For God so loved the world
that He gave His one and only Son,
that whoever believes in Him shall not perish
but have eternal life.

JOHN 3:16 NIV

God loves us, He treasures us,
and He delights in our existence.

MELISSA HORVATH

For more inspiration, scan here:

I PRAYED FOR YOU JUST NOW AND ASKED GOD TO REMIND YOU THAT HE'S *cheering you on!*

The LORD your God is with you,
the Mighty Warrior who saves.
He will take great delight in you;
in His love He will no longer rebuke you,
but will rejoice over you with singing.

ZEPHANIAH 3:17 NIV

Instead of having doubt,
have trust in the One Most High.

MELISSA HORVATH

For more inspiration, scan here:

TODAY I PRAYED YOU'LL BE REMINDED THAT YOU DON'T HAVE TO RELY ON YOUR OWN

strength.

GOD IS WITH YOU.

He gives strength to the weary and increases the power of the weak. Even youths grow tired and weary, and young men stumble and fall; but those who hope in the LORD will renew their strength.

ISAIAH 40:29–31 NIV

Let God's strength wash over you and build you so that you will be fully prepared for whatever comes your way.

MELISSA HORVATH

For more
inspiration,
scan here:

I ASKED GOD TO REMIND YOU TODAY THAT HE WILL MEET

every

SINGLE NEED, NO MATTER HOW LARGE OR SMALL.

And God is able to bless you abundantly,
so that in all things at all times,
having all that you need,
you will abound in every good work.

II CORINTHIANS 9:8 NIV

God provides a way when we feel there is no other way—when it seems that all the doors and windows are closed.

MELISSA HORVATH

DaySpring

For more inspiration, scan here:

I ASKED GOD TO REMIND YOU THAT LIFE MOVES IN

seasons.

WHAT SEASON ARE YOU IN TODAY?

There is a time for everything,
and everything on earth
has its special season.

ECCLESIASTES 3:1 NCV

The sun will still come up tomorrow, and God provides a fresh start.

MELISSA HORVATH

For more
inspiration,
scan here:

I PRAYED FOR YOU AND SPECIFICALLY ASKED GOD TO BRING

contentment

TO YOUR WEARY HEART.

Serving God does make us very rich,
if we are satisfied with what we have.

I TIMOTHY 6:6 NCV

If we allow ourselves to believe the world's lie, we will never have the peace or contentment that comes with understanding how valuable we are in God's eyes.

MELISSA HORVATH

For more
inspiration,
scan here:

TODAY I ASKED GOD TO REMOVE FEAR FROM YOUR HEART. HE CAN ERASE FEARS AND REPLACE THEM WITH PEACE IF YOU WEAR HIS MIGHTY

armor.

Therefore put on the full armor of God, so that when the day of evil comes, you may be able to stand your ground, and after you have done everything, to stand.

EPHESIANS 6:13 NIV

When you start to fear, put on the armor of God.

MELISSA HORVATH

For more inspiration, scan here:

WHAT ARE YOU WAITING FOR? YOU CAN BE *happy* TODAY, NO MATTER WHAT YOU'RE GOING THROUGH!

Consider it pure joy, my brothers and sisters,
whenever you face trials of many kinds, because you know
that the testing of your faith produces perseverance.
Let perseverance finish its work so that you may be mature
and complete, not lacking anything.

JAMES 1:2–4 NIV

Let God guide you in the waiting.
Ask Him to give you an extra dose of patience and love.

MELISSA HORVATH

I PRAYED THAT GOD WOULD HELP YOU WITH YOUR NEGATIVE THOUGHTS. THEY *don't* HAVE TO CONSUME YOU.

Set your minds on things above, not on earthly things.

COLOSSIANS 3:2 NIV

When the walls are in front of us and there's no way out, prayer breaks through all walls.

MELISSA HORVATH

DaySpring

For more
inspiration,
scan here:

I PRAYED FOR YOU TO TAKE *chances!*

GOD HAS BIG THINGS FOR YOU TO DO.

This is why I remind you to keep using the gift God gave you when I laid my hands on you. Now let it grow, as a small flame grows into a fire. God did not give us a spirit that makes us afraid but a spirit of power and love and self-control.

II TIMOTHY 1:6–7 NCV

Do a new thing today and step out in faith . . . get out of your comfort zone and start saying yes to the callings God placed on your heart.

MELISSA HORVATH

For more
inspiration,
scan here:

I ASKED GOD TO REMIND YOU THAT HE

knew and loved

YOU EVEN BEFORE YOU WERE BORN.

My frame was not hidden from You when I was made in the secret place, when I was woven together in the depths of the earth. Your eyes saw my unformed body; all the days ordained for me were written in Your book before one of them came to be.

PSALM 139:15–16 NIV

Isn't it wonderful to think that we were each uniquely created by the One Most High? He planned for you specifically even before you were born!

MELISSA HORVATH

For more
inspiration,
scan here:

I PRAY THAT YOU'LL SEE THAT GOD'S *power* IS AT WORK INSIDE OF YOU, AND IT'S BIGGER THAN ANY PROBLEMS YOU MIGHT FACE.

For it is God who works in you
to will and to act in order to fulfill
His good purpose.

PHILIPPIANS 2:13 NIV

But rest assured, God is always working. There is a special purpose in each season, even when we can't see what it is.

MELISSA HORVATH

For more inspiration, scan here:

I PRAY YOU'LL REMEMBER THAT SOMETIMES

less is more.

GOD IS ALREADY PREPARING YOU FOR WHAT'S COMING NEXT!

Humble yourselves, therefore,
under the mighty hand of God
so that at the proper time he may exalt you,
casting all your anxieties on him,
because he cares for you.

I PETER 5:6–7 ESV

God is there with us in the waiting,
guiding us and preparing us
for what He has planned.

MELISSA HORVATH

For more
inspiration,
scan here:

TODAY I PRAYED THAT GOD WOULD GIVE YOU

confidence and joy,

NO MATTER WHAT YOU'RE FACING.

For the LORD *will be your confidence*
and will keep your foot from being caught.

PROVERBS 3:26 ESV

Give your fears and worries to God!
He can silence the fear in our mind
as we grow our confidence in Him.

MELISSA HORVATH

DaySpring

For more inspiration, scan here:

I ASKED GOD TO POINT OUT SOMEONE IN YOUR PATH TODAY WHO NEEDS YOUR

Smile

AND

ENCOURAGEMENT.

Bear one another's burdens,
and so fulfill the law of Christ.

GALATIANS 6:2 ESV

When we help others and receive help ourselves, we can lessen our stress and feel good about helping those in need.

MELISSA HORVATH

For more
inspiration,
scan here:

I PRAYED THAT GOD WOULD REMIND YOU THAT

SUCCESSES

ARE COMING!

Delight yourself in the LORD,
and he will give you the desires of your heart.

PSALM 37:4 ESV

Try to remember to thank God for eliminating the roadblocks, guiding you to success, and opening the right doors at the right time.

MELISSA HORVATH

For more
inspiration,
scan here:

TODAY I PRAYED THAT YOU WOULD LET GOD LIFT THOSE *weights* SO THAT YOU DON'T HAVE TO CARRY THEM ALONE.

But to all who did receive him,
who believed in his name,
he gave the right to become children of God.

JOHN 1:12 ESV

There are seasons of life when we do carry a lot, but seek out what you enjoy and see what you can take off your plate or what can be done differently to bring more time to your day.

MELISSA HORVATH

DaySpring

For more inspiration, scan here:

I PRAY THE LORD
GIVES YOU THE
courage
TO LEAD THE WAY,
YOUR LIGHT
SHINING BRIGHT.

*Finally, be strong in the Lord
and in the strength of his might.*

EPHESIANS 6:10 ESV

**Do not be afraid.
You are strong and courageous!
Let the strength God has provided you
to shine through!**

MELISSA HORVATH

For more
inspiration,
scan here:

TODAY I PRAYED THAT GOD WOULD MAKE YOU AS

AS A LION!

Since we have such a hope,
we are very bold.

II CORINTHIANS 3:12 ESV

Fight the urge to stay in your mold; break through and experience the goodness God has in store for you.

MELISSA HORVATH

DaySpring

For more inspiration, scan here:

I PRAY THAT GOD REMINDS YOU TODAY THAT HE IS A

waymaker,

A MIRACLE WORKER, A PROMISE KEEPER.

You are the God of miracles and wonders!
You still demonstrate Your awesome power.

PSALM 77:14 TLB

God is the way maker.
He may open a way for you to move,
and it will be up to you to take action,
even if it's a huge change
or makes you feel totally uncomfortable.

MELISSA HORVATH

DaySpring

For more
inspiration,
scan here:

I PRAYED THAT YOU WOULD FEEL

settled

AND PEACEFUL.

Now may the Lord of peace Himself
give you peace at all times and in every way.
The Lord be with all of you.

II THESSALONIANS 3:16 NIV

When you are aligned with God,
using the gifts He gave you to share His love,
you'll find that life falls into place
and that peace will reside in your heart.

MELISSA HORVATH

For more
inspiration,
scan here:

TODAY I PRAYED THAT GOD WOULD GIVE YOU COMPLETE HEALTH AND *wholeness.*

Gracious words are like a honeycomb,
sweetness to the soul and health to the body.

PROVERBS 16:24 ESV

What if we started living in the yes by saying yes to ourselves and our health and no to what depletes us?

MELISSA HORVATH

For more
inspiration,
scan here:

I PRAYED THAT GOD WOULD REMIND YOU THAT HE'S ALREADY

hard at work

ON YOUR BEHALF.

For it is God who works in you,
both to will and to work for his good pleasure.

PHILIPPIANS 2:13 ESV

God is writing all our stories;
in fact, even before you were born,
your story was written.

MELISSA HORVATH

For more
inspiration,
scan here:

I SAID A PRAYER THAT YOU WOULD BE REMINDED OF YOUR VALUE. YOU ARE A RARE

jewel.

I delight greatly in the LORD; my soul rejoices in my God. For He has clothed me with garments of salvation and arrayed me in a robe of His righteousness, as a bridegroom adorns his head like a priest, and as a bride adorns herself with her jewels.

ISAIAH 61:10 NIV

Our lives aren't defined by our titles but by what Jesus says we are. And He says that we are loved, cared for, and valued.

MELISSA HORVATH

For more
inspiration,
scan here:

I'M PRAYING FOR *Success* IN ALL YOU DO TODAY.

May He give you the desire of your heart and make all your plans succeed.

PSALM 20:4 NIV

Power doesn't equal happiness, and neither does money.

MELISSA HORVATH

For more
inspiration,
scan here:

TODAY I'M PRAYING
YOU WILL SEE YOURSELF
AS AN

Overcomer

IN ALL
YOU'RE FACING.

But thanks be to God,
who gives us the victory
through our Lord Jesus Christ.

I CORINTHIANS 15:57 ESV

Just as parents celebrate their children's victories—
a first step or an A on a report card—
God celebrates our victories too.

MELISSA HORVATH

For more
inspiration,
scan here:

MAY THE LORD

bless you

AND KEEP YOU.
MAY HIS FACE SHINE
UPON YOU AND GIVE
YOU PEACE.

And the peace of God,
which transcends all understanding,
will guard your hearts and your minds
in Christ Jesus.

PHILIPPIANS 4:7 NIV

When you are aligned with God, using the gifts He gave you to share His love, you'll find that life falls into place and that peace will reside in your heart.

MELISSA HORVATH

For more
inspiration,
scan here:

I PRAYED THAT JOY WOULD BUBBLE UP INSIDE OF YOU LIKE A *fountain.*

But let all who take refuge in You be glad; let them ever sing for joy. Spread Your protection over them, that those who love Your name may rejoice in You.

PSALM 5:11 NIV

Free yourself from the many titles you have and the multitude of tasks on your plate today, and do something that brings you joy.

MELISSA HORVATH

For more inspiration, scan here:

TODAY I ASKED GOD
TO REMIND YOU
THAT YOU
belong
TO HIM.
YOU ARE HIS
PRECIOUS CHILD.

*The Spirit Himself
testifies with our spirit
that we are God's children.*

ROMANS 8:16 NIV

**Instead of thinking you've been forgotten,
remember that God has
your best interests in mind.**

MELISSA HORVATH

For more
inspiration,
scan here:

I PRAYED THAT YOU WOULD *go easy* ON YOURSELF TODAY.

If we confess our sins, He is faithful and just and will forgive us our sins and purify us from all unrighteousness.

1 JOHN 1:9 NIV

When you slow things down and don't put so much pressure on yourself, you'll find more peace, and that's what God longs for us to have— His peace inside and outside ourselves.

MELISSA HORVATH

For more
inspiration,
scan here:

I ASKED GOD TO REMIND YOU THAT THE BATTLE HAS ALREADY BEEN

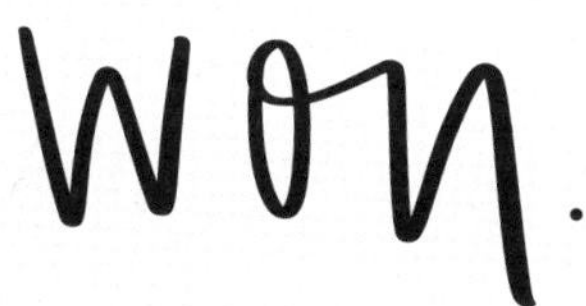

He rescues me unharmed
from the battle waged against me,
even though many oppose me.

PSALM 55:18 NIV

The good news is, we already know that the battle has been won! Good wins over evil. God wants us to live in a posture of peace instead of worry and tribulation.

MELISSA HORVATH

DaySpring

For more
inspiration,
scan here:

I'M PRAYING YOU WILL HAVE THE COURAGE TO

let go

OF THE THINGS THAT HAVE BEEN HOLDING YOU BACK.

Brothers and sisters, I do not consider myself yet to have taken hold of it. But one thing I do: Forgetting what is behind and straining toward what is ahead, I press on toward the goal to win the prize for which God has called me heavenward in Christ Jesus.

PHILIPPIANS 3:13–14 NIV

The past is the past. God wants you to look forward, to the light of Jesus, not stay in the shadows.

MELISSA HORVATH

For more
inspiration,
scan here:

I PRAYED FOR GOD'S

supernatural

peace

TO COMPLETELY ENVELOP YOU TODAY.

May God Himself, the God of peace, sanctify you through and through. May your whole spirit, soul and body be kept blameless at the coming of our Lord Jesus Christ.

I THESSALONIAN 5:23 NIV

Even watching the ocean or a campfire
can be soothing to the soul.
What do you enjoy doing?
What recharges your soul?

MELISSA HORVATH

DaySpring

For more
inspiration,
scan here:

TODAY I ASKED GOD TO REMIND YOU THAT HE GIVES YOU *everything* YOU NEED.

For nothing will be impossible with God.

LUKE 1:37 ESV

God created you for many wonderful purposes in life. He is equipping you today to fulfill the amazing plans He has for you!

MELISSA HORVATH

For more
inspiration,
scan here:

I PRAYED THAT YOU WOULD REMEMBER HOW

beautiful

YOU ARE.

So God created man in his own image,
in the image of God he created him;
male and female he created them.

GENESIS 1:27 ESV

God says that you are beautiful—inside and out.
He says you are one of a kind.
He treasures you, He values you,
and He created you in His image.

MELISSA HORVATH

For more
inspiration,
scan here:

I PRAY THE LORD *inspires* YOU WITH NEW, CREATIVE IDEAS TODAY.

Each of you should use whatever gift you have received to serve others, as faithful stewards of God's grace in its various forms.

I PETER 4:10 NIV

God gave you wonderful and beautiful talents for you to put your unique stamp on the world and do what you were meant to do.

MELISSA HORVATH

DaySpring

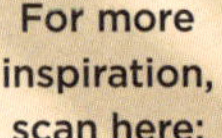
For more
inspiration,
scan here:

I PRAYED TODAY FOR COMPLETE *provision,* THAT ALL OF YOUR NEEDS WOULD BE MET—AND THEN SOME!

I was young and now I am old,
yet I have never seen the righteous forsaken
or their children begging bread.

PSALM 37:25 NIV

Looking back on your younger years, don't you wish that you hadn't worried about how God would provide for you? Look how far you've come! Have faith!

MELISSA HORVATH

For more inspiration, scan here:

TODAY I PRAYED THAT GOD WOULD REMIND YOU THAT HE IS YOUR GOOD *shepherd*, TENDING TO YOUR EVERY NEED.

"I am the good shepherd.
The good shepherd lays down
His life for the sheep."

JOHN 10:11 NIV

We are the sheep,
and Jesus is the Shepherd.
He watches over us and sits at the door,
making sure that we're safe.

MELISSA HORVATH

For more inspiration, scan here:

I PRAYED FOR YOU TODAY, THAT YOU WOULDN'T quit.

Make sure that your endurance carries you all the way without failing, so that you may be perfect and complete, lacking nothing.

JAMES 1:4 GNT

God reminds us in Galatians that our good works are not for nothing—and that we shouldn't give up doing good things just because we don't get an instant reward.

MELISSA HORVATH

DaySpring

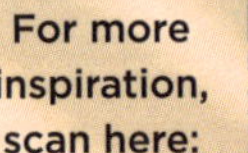
For more
inspiration,
scan here:

I PRAYED THAT THE LORD WOULD REMIND YOU THAT THE PROBLEMS YOU'RE FACING ARE

temporary.

And this small and temporary trouble we suffer will bring us a tremendous and eternal glory, much greater than the trouble.

II CORINTHIANS 4:17 GNT

If we never go through hard times, we'll hardly notice when good ones come.

MELISSA HORVATH

DaySpring

For more inspiration, scan here:

I PRAYED THAT YOU WOULD BE FILLED WITH

encouragement

TODAY.

You, LORD, hear the desire of the afflicted;
You encourage them,
and You listen to their cry.

PSALM 10:17 NIV

Let His Word give you strength and encouragement
when you need it the most.
When you walk with God continuously,
you'll remember He's already there
when both the good and bad times come.

MELISSA HORVATH

For more
inspiration,
scan here:

TODAY I ASKED GOD TO REMIND YOU THAT YOU

don't

HAVE TO BE PERFECT.

HE LOVES YOU JUST AS YOU ARE!

For all have sinned and fall short of the glory of God.

ROMANS 3:23 NIV

How can you start practicing being present in your life instead of striving for perfection, which is a hill we cannot climb? When we realize that we are imperfect beings, we can rest assured that there is a perfect Someone who is making our paths straight.

MELISSA HORVATH

For more inspiration, scan here:

TODAY I PRAYED THAT YOU WOULD BE REMINDED THAT, EVEN THOUGH LIFE IS HARD, GOD IS

good.

I believe that I shall look upon
the goodness of the LORD
in the land of the living!

PSALM 27:13 ESV

Fight the urge to stay in your mold;
break through and experience the goodness
He has in store for you.

MELISSA HORVATH

For more
inspiration,
scan here:

I PRAYED FOR YOU TODAY, THAT YOUR *faith* WOULD GROW STRONGER AND STRONGER.

Now faith is confidence in what we hope for
and assurance about what we do not see.

HEBREWS 11:1 NIV

Let God work and change your heart
to look to the light
and the goodness through Him.

MELISSA HORVATH

DaySpring

For more inspiration, scan here:

TODAY I PRAYED THAT YOU WOULD BE ABLE TO REST IN GOD'S

presence.

When you draw close to God,
God will draw close to you.

JAMES 4:8 TLB

Taking time away with God is not selfish; it's a necessary means for you to recharge and stay aligned with God's plan and purpose for your life.

MELISSA HORVATH

For more
inspiration,
scan here:

I PRAYED FOR YOU, THAT YOU WOULD BE ABLE TO HANDLE LIFE'S

changes

WITH EASE.

For we walk by faith, not by sight.

II CORINTHIANS 5:7 ESV

If God is calling you to do it and you don't move as you should, you'll miss all the wonderful things He has in store for you!

MELISSA HORVATH

For more
inspiration,
scan here:

TODAY I PRAYED THAT GOD WOULD

soothe

ALL OF YOUR FEARS WITH HIS LIFE-GIVING WORDS.

The L*ORD* *is my light and my salvation—*
whom shall I fear?
The L*ORD* *is the stronghold of my life—*
of whom shall I be afraid?

PSALM 27:1 NIV

Most of the things we worry about never happen. Let God's life-giving words soothe your fears.

MELISSA HORVATH

For more
inspiration,
scan here:

I PRAYED THAT THE LORD WOULD REMIND YOU THAT HE'S IN THE

rescue

BUSINESS.

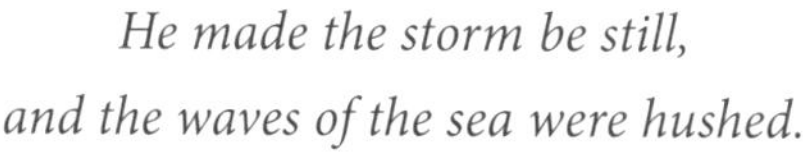

He made the storm be still,
and the waves of the sea were hushed.

PSALM 107:29 ESV

God is stronger and His plans are greater than any storm we face on earth.

MELISSA HORVATH

DaySpring

For more
inspiration,
scan here:

TODAY I PRAYED THAT THE LORD WOULD GIVE YOU

courage

TO TAKE CHANCES.

David also said to Solomon his son,
"Be strong and courageous, and do the work.
Do not be afraid or discouraged,
for the LORD *God, my God, is with you.*
He will not fail you or forsake you
until all the work for the service
of the temple of the LORD *is finished."*

I CHRONICLES 28:20 NIV

Work hard, but remember the One who got you where you are today!

MELISSA HORVATH

DaySpring

For more
inspiration,
scan here:

I ASKED GOD
TO REMIND YOU
THAT YOU ARE
uniquely
YOU . . .
FOR A REASON!

Your hands made me and formed me;
give me understanding to learn Your commands.
May those who fear You rejoice when they see me,
for I have put my hope in Your word.

PSALM 119:73–74 NIV

We all have been given different
talents and unique characteristics.
There was never anyone like you ever before,
and there never will be again.

MELISSA HORVATH

For more inspiration, scan here:

TODAY I
ASKED GOD TO
stir up
THE GIFTS, TALENTS,
AND ABILITIES
HE HAS PLACED
INSIDE OF YOU.

We have different gifts,
according to the grace given to each of us.

ROMANS 12:6 NIV

What's keeping you from taking the next step
toward something you were made to do,
something that will bring you joy,
or something that aligns
with your God-given gifts?

MELISSA HORVATH

DaySpring

TODAY I PRAY
YOU CAN TAKE A
moment
TO JUST BE.

My soul thirsts for God, for the living God.
When can I go and meet with God?

PSALM 42:2 NIV

Today and every day, try to be still
to let the Holy Spirit speak to and guide you.
If you feel as if you haven't heard from God,
pray that He will reveal Himself to you.

MELISSA HORVATH

For more
inspiration,
scan here:

I PRAYED THAT YOU WOULD BE REMINDED THAT GOD

welcomes

YOU WITH OPEN ARMS, NO MATTER WHAT.

There is no fear in love.
But perfect love drives out fear,
because fear has to do with punishment.
The one who fears
is not made perfect in love.

I JOHN 4:18 NIV

God doesn't want you to punish yourself or feel like you're not good enough for Him. He knew you before you were born, and He loves you just as you are!

MELISSA HORVATH

DaySpring

For more inspiration, scan here:

TODAY I PRAYED THAT ANY OF YOUR ANXIETIES WOULD

flee,

LIKE A BIRD TAKING FLIGHT.

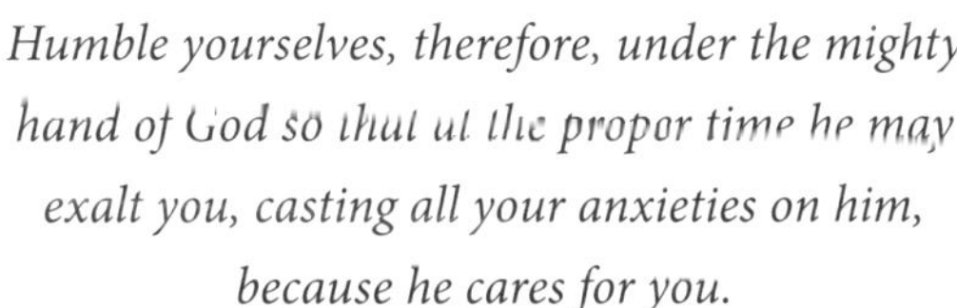

Humble yourselves, therefore, under the mighty hand of God so that at the proper time he may exalt you, casting all your anxieties on him, because he cares for you.

I PETER 5:6–7 ESV

When you find yourself letting fear and anxiety creep into situations you're struggling to deal with, remember what God wants us to know from His Word. Let His powerful words wash over you and calm you.

MELISSA HORVATH

For more
inspiration,
scan here:

I PRAYED THAT GOD WOULD REMIND YOU THAT HE CAN

Meet you

IN THE INTERRUPTIONS OF LIFE.

Blessed is the one who perseveres under trial because, having stood the test, that person will receive the crown of life that the Lord has promised to those who love Him.

JAMES 1:12 NIV

When you lean on God and know that He has your best interests in mind, you'll be able to ease through times of trials.

MELISSA HORVATH

TODAY I PRAYED
GOD WOULD WHISPER
THE WORDS,
"go for it!"
IN YOUR EAR.

I will instruct you and teach you
in the way you should go;
I will counsel you
with my eye upon you.

PSALM 32:8 ESV

What's been on your heart or mind lately to pursue?
What's stopping you from making the next move?

MELISSA HORVATH

DaySpring

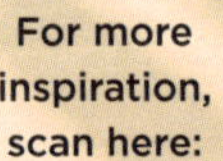
For more
inspiration,
scan here:

I'M PRAYING FOR YOU, THAT YOU WILL EXPERIENCE GOD'S *blessings* AT EVERY TURN.

Praise be to the God and Father
of our Lord Jesus Christ,
who has blessed us in the heavenly realms
with every spiritual blessing in Christ.

EPHESIANS 1:3 NIV

Try looking at things outside of what's causing the stress, and count the blessings around you.

MELISSA HORVATH

For more
inspiration,
scan here:

I PRAYED THAT GOD WOULD GIVE YOU THE COURAGE TO

speak up

WHEN THE SITUATION CALLS FOR IT.

"The good person out of the good treasure of his heart produces good, and the evil person out of his evil treasure produces evil, for out of the abundance of the heart his mouth speaks."

LUKE 6:45 ESV

When we speak the truth, our heart is filled with the light and love of Jesus.

MELISSA HORVATH

For more
inspiration,
scan here:

I PRAYED THAT
GOD WOULD GIVE YOU
THE COURAGE TO
let go
OF THE REINS
AND HAND THEM
TO HIM.

"Have I not commanded you? Be strong and courageous.
Do not be frightened, and do not be dismayed,
for the LORD *your God is with you wherever you go."*

JOSHUA 1:9 ESV

The next time an obstacle comes your way,
practice not fretting about it.
Instead, remember that God's got this!

MELISSA HORVATH

For more
inspiration,
scan here:

MY PRAYER TODAY IS THAT YOU WOULD COME TO FULLY UNDERSTAND JUST HOW

adored

YOU ARE BY THE ONE WHO CREATED YOU.

So we have come to know and to believe the love that God has for us. God is love, and whoever abides in love abides in God, and God abides in him.

I JOHN 4:16 ESV

God loves you beyond measure.
He knows how many hairs are on your head.
He knows what's best for you,
even if you can't see it yet.

MELISSA HORVATH

For more
inspiration,
scan here:

TODAY I PRAYED THAT YOU WOULD BE ABLE TO

Step away

FROM THE BUSYNESS OF LIFE AND ENJOY SOME QUIET TIME WITH THE LORD.

It is in vain that you rise up early and
go late to rest, eating the bread of anxious toil;
for he gives to his beloved sleep.

PSALM 127:2 ESV

If you feel like you haven't heard from the Holy Spirit, pray for God to reveal Himself to you and to heighten your spiritual senses so you can see and hear from Him today.

MELISSA HORVATH

I'M PRAYING THAT YOU WILL REMEMBER ONE KEY FACT: GOD'S TIMING IS *perfect!*

But I trust in you, O LORD;
I say, "You are my God."
My times are in your hand.

PSALM 31:14–15 ESV

What if we stop wishing away time and start trusting the One who holds the universe together? We can trust in His perfect timing and know that His timing is better than we can ever imagine.

MELISSA HORVATH

DaySpring

I PRAY YOU WOULD BE REMINDED TODAY THAT GOD WOULDN'T CALL YOU TO IT IF HE DIDN'T PLAN TO

equip

YOU FOR IT.

For who is God, but the LORD?
And who is a rock, except our God?—
the God who equipped me with strength
and made my way blameless.

PSALM 18:31–32 ESV

Look ahead to the great things God has in store for you.

MELISSA HORVATH

DaySpring

For more
inspiration,
scan here: